"Process-Skipping": A Mechanism That Locks In Addictive Patterns and Blocks the Experience of Grace

Edwin M. McMahon, Ph.D.
Peter A. Campbell, Ph.D.

Sheed & Ward

Sheed & Ward™ is a service of National Catholic Reporter Publishing Company, Inc.

ISBN: 1-55612-513-5

Published by: Sheed & Ward
115 E. Armour Blvd. P.O. Box 419492
Kansas City, MO 64141-6492

To order, call: (800) 333-7373

"Process-Skipping": A Mechanism That Locks In Addictive Patterns and Blocks the Experience of Grace

In this booklet we want to provide you with practical criteria that can help you better evaluate the psychological soundness of spiritual growth practices. There is currently such a bewildering array of different approaches available through growth centers and retreat houses that it is often difficult to choose from among the vast collection of eastern, western and contemporary offerings. Developing critical norms for evaluating how psychologically helpful any of these practices may be is essential when you consider the amount of time and effort required on your part to become proficient in any given system. The potential for re-enforcing addictive tendencies inherent within many so-called "growth" and "spiritual" practices is enormous.

What we offer in the following pages are some easily recognizable clues drawn from our research that will help you evaluate such practices for your own personal use or, if you happen to be a retreat house director or spiritual guide, will provide criteria that can be useful in evaluating a wide range of approaches for the benefit of those whom you serve.

Introduction

Let's begin by examining how we all spontaneously try to develop effective ways of dealing with difficult feelings that get in the way of personal and spiritual growth. Feelings, of course, are only one aspect of the broader subject of spiritual life. However, they are important not only because we all have troublesome feelings and invariably use religious or spiritual practices to cope with them, but also because feelings put us in touch with our bodies, and body-knowing is the most neglected aspect of current Western spirituality.

Have you ever stopped to consider that behind whatever effort you make to change your negative feelings, there lies an entire set of inbuilt "assumptions" about how such difficult feelings can develop into something better? For most of us, these assumptions are uncritically accepted. As a small child, whenever you felt something you didn't like, that scared or hurt in some way, you immediately wanted to change it. Probably, you looked around to see how your parents, brothers and sisters or children at school tried to change or cope with difficult feelings and then you copied them. After that, a pattern set in which most likely you have followed to this day.

As a child, you didn't have the background to evaluate whatever approach you chanced upon. But even as adults trying to improve upon our methods of change, most of us still lack the knowledge to assess what is being proposed to us.

As a step toward becoming more informed in this area, then, let's first examine how people change and grow in a psychological process that supports the integration of the whole human organism—namely, *Focusing.* We will then contrast this experience with a popular and erroneous assumption about how feelings change which frustrates many of our efforts to grow.

Eugene Gendlin: Focusing

A broad underlying principle guides Dr. Eugene Gendlin's analysis of how feelings unfold as well as how the Focusing process actually works:

> *Every "bad" feeling is potential energy toward a more right way of being if you give it space to move toward its rightness.*[1]

This simple, direct statement has emerged from a long history of clinical observation and experimentation begun by Eugene Gendlin's teacher and colleague, Dr. Carl Rogers, and carried further forward by Gendlin himself. In this view, negative feelings are not some sort of enemy to be conquered and eliminated. Rather, they contain special indicators of the unique direction for growth within each person. Both Rogers and Gendlin realized that *congruence* with one's own feelings and process of experiencing was crucial for successful change and growth. By congruence we mean being able consciously to feel our feelings physiologically and allow them to symbolize themselves accurately. For Gendlin, Focusing was an effective way to become congruent by remaining in touch with a bodily-felt tendency toward wholeness.

> The very existence of bad feelings within you is evidence that your body knows what is wrong and what is right. It must know what it would be like to feel perfect, or it could not evoke a sense of wrong. The bad feeling is the body knowing and pushing toward what good would be.

> The feelings of 'bad' or 'wrong' inside you are, in effect, your body's measurement of the distance between 'perfect' and the way it actually feels. It knows the direction. It knows this just as surely as you know which way to move a crooked picture. If the crookedness is pronounced enough for you to notice it at all, there is absolutely no chance that you will move the picture in the wrong direction and make it still more crooked while mistaking that for straight. *The sense of what is wrong carries with it, inseparably, a sense of the direction toward what is right.* (emphasis ours)[2]

For Gendlin, when difficult feelings are a problem, the principal resource and starting point for change is the body-sense of what is wrong. *It is never some ideal "opposite" of the painful way in which you find yourself, as our religious and cultural conditioning so often suggest.*

There is an erroneous assumption in any approach to change which bypasses a congruent presence to difficult feelings and instead concentrates attention upon some imagined ideal that one seeks to draw strength from or substitute in place of whatever troubles us. Such effort invariably results in a lack of "congruence"—the not "owning" of what is real in ourselves. Incongruence refers to a condition of out-of-touchness with your bodily-felt experiencing. There is a fundamental discrepancy between how you actually feel in any given situation and the way you represent that situation in your awareness.

As we shall show in a moment, such out-of-touchness is the psychological underpinning for most addiction. Addictive behavior is an incongruent person's substitute for genuine presence to his or her felt experience. When culture or religion lead you away from your actual feelings by substituting something else in their place, that culture and religion are already innately addictive in themselves and will, in an enabling way, foster and support addictive religious behavior.

We must never underestimate the pervasive reach of that erroneous assumption which teaches people to aim at some positive characteristic as the way to change or overcome unacceptable feelings. So often family, culture and religion teach that if you're angry, you should strive for compassion; when timid, master the art of self assertion; if sad, entertain happy thoughts and memories.

Take, for example, the following prayer experience, suggested as a way to let go of bitterness over past hurt. The author begins by having you relax and recall scenes from your past where you were hurt. He first invites you to imagine taking the offending person by the hand and telling him or her that you forgive them.

> Each time you use this prayer experience, you can imagine different scenes and different people.
>
> As some of the people pass before your mind's eye you will feel uncomfortable telling them, 'I forgive you.' The hurts are held so deeply that it is difficult for you to let go of them. Father Anthony DeMello, in his . . . book, *Sadhana,* . . . suggests the following way of letting go of deep hurt and unforgiveness.
>
> First, imagine that you see Jesus Christ on the cross. Take whatever time you might need to have a sense of Him on the cross.
>
> Now turn to the scene of pain where you are hurt and stay with that scene for a while. Keep alternating between the picture of Jesus on the cross and the scene of your hurt. Soon you will find your resentment slipping away from you, and a feeling of peace and joy will sweep over you. A feeling of lightheartedness will overcome you as the image of Our Lord on the cross enables you to let go of imbedded hurt.[3]

In this example, the image of Christ on the cross, together with all the feelings generated through contemplation of this sacred event are used as the resource, the catalyst for change, the power *apart from* bitterness and hurt that is used to overcome them.

There are, no doubt, limited circumstances where such an experience might benefit someone whose anger or bitterness is sufficiently mild that they can separate their hurt from the person who has offended them, forgiving the person before assuming responsibility to let their hurt unfold and tell its story. However, when they have been "hooked" by their bitterness to the point where they cannot let go of it, as seems to be the case in the preceding exercise, then we must be critical both of the psychological inaccuracy and potential for addiction in such an approach. There is also the undermining potential for "shaming with guilt" present in this exercise. "How can you continue to hold on to your anger when Christ has suffered so much for you and loves the person whom you hate?"

Eugene Gendlin's research at the University of Chicago clearly shows that negative feelings change when such transformation is rooted in a "graced," bodily-felt process. He does not fall into the trap of a "cognitive or emotional balancing act" which suggests that if there is darkness, equalize it with light! Your mind may like to think this way but your body-knowing does not move forward in this fashion.

It is a totally false assumption to imagine that we gain power over what we regard as a "bad feeling" by using either a "good thought" or a "good feeling" to achieve this goal. All one accomplishes with such futile exercise is to re-enforce his or her own lack of congruence. When this happens, we become even more vulnerable to nameless anxiety and the breakdown of whatever charade we happen to be playing in order to remain out of touch with real feelings.

The prayer exercise just described is psychologically impotent for allowing feelings of hurt and bitterness to tell their own stories and unfold into something better. The author of this passage does not begin and remain with the hurt and bitterness. He doesn't look for the saving presence of Christ and the direction toward wholeness right within the felt experience of bitterness itself. Rather, he has us alternate attention between a bad feeling from the past and a more positive inspirational awareness drawn from the contemplation of Christ on the cross. The positive feeling is intended to be used as a way to counter-condition the painful memory.

It would be far more accurate psychologically as well as theologically to seek the saving presence of Christ on the cross *right within the painful bitterness itself.* The bodily-felt unfolding of such bitterness into more positive feelings through a gift of healing grace brings the person at prayer into an actual experience within his or her own body of the renewing Paschal Mystery, the death and resurrection of Christ.

Gendlin's research indicates that it is an erroneous psychological assumption to believe that we must look apart from the negative feeling itself in order to discover some kind of resolution. This vital learning provides an important criterion for evaluating spiritual and growth practices. Does the approach begin and remain with our real feelings until they unfold, or does it seek, rather, to direct attention toward some ideal opposite feeling that you are told to substitute for whatever troubles you?

It seems almost foreign, doesn't it, to start and stay with what we want to get rid of? Our natural tendency is to look for resolution *apart from* what we don't like or cannot accept in ourselves. The reason for this is because we instinctively try to gain power over what pains us. That means finding some resource with greater energy than the difficult feeling, something apart from it that can motivate, inspire, and help us do battle with the enemy in ourselves.

This is a basic cultural "assumption" we all have learned about how feelings change, and the assumption permeates most religious practices in our Western tradition as well. But such a "power trip" has nothing to do with spiritual growth. Indeed, it is the direct antithesis of any psychological process that disposes us for grace. Counter-conditioning is just one more attempt at control, even when couched in religious language. We are slow to realize that this false assumption has destroyed more human lives and thwarted the sincere aspirations of more religious people than we will ever imagine. It is a psychological and theological cancer more virulent in its social consequences than any disease of the physical organism.

L.L. Whyte: "unitary consciousness"

During the Second World War, while the Nazis were busy bombing London and other major cities in England, a British physicist-philosopher took refuge in the English countryside to compose a definitive lifework about the evolutionary next phase in human development. His book[4] was destined to influence many subsequent thinkers, including Carl Rogers and, through him, Eugene Gendlin. Lancelot Law Whyte's work has been described as a penetrating analysis of the kind of civilization human beings must build if they are to survive on this planet. The subject matter he wrote about while bombs fell nearby and most of Europe went up in flames dealt with the exact same problem we are now discussing!

Whyte realized that unless an entirely new form of consciousness emerged within the human species, it would be doomed to escalate past conflicts into some form of catastrophic future holocaust that could well destroy civilization as we know it. He named the needed new awareness "unitary consciousness" and distinguished it from "dissociated" forms of awareness.

In Whyte's view, the unitary person is "congruent," to use our term, welcoming development and personal transformation. A dissociated individual, on the other hand, fears the imagined insecurity of such change and substitutes *the pursuit of ideals* in its place. The dissociated person is "incongruent," out of touch with the meaning of his or her felt experience and wracked with all the anxieties that accompany such a divided way of living. Rather than face the imagined terror of actually opening to one's inner pain and hurt (Step #4 of the Focusing Process—"Letting go into it, just being in it, sensing the whole of it"), such an individual escapes into an addictive quest for solace by trying to acquire some shining quality that can overpower his or her inner demon. Whyte's devastating philosophical critique of this vain pursuit of ideals exposes a fatal flaw in many practices of the Christian religion as well.

> The failure of idealistic thought lay partly in the fact that it did not recognize that every ideal is linked to its shadow. The Chris-

tian cross is a symbol not only of the compassion of Jesus, but of the sadism which he provoked. This ambivalence, which appears paradoxical to minds trained in a static rationalism, is an elementary consequence of process thought. If a formative process is divided, it falls into contrasted components. Whatever is incomplete is thus always complemented by its contrary; *the penalty for any principle which fails to express the whole is the necessity to co-exist with its opposite* (emphasis ours). Partial love implies partial hate; spirit, sensuality; self-sacrificing compassion, sadism. The denial of any aspect sharpens and preserves it, while its acceptance transforms it by bringing it within the process of the whole. By proclaiming the ideal of universal compassion, the dissociated Christian tends to neglect the complementary fact of the sadism of every dissociated nature. The more romantic the worship of compassion, the deeper must be the division and the suppressed sadism.

> If suppression implied disappearance, the history of Europe would have been different. But ideals which seek to deny their shadows eventually exhaust their own power, when the dissociated balance becomes unstable and the dark component seizes control.[5]

This is the tragic consequence of any attempt to control negative feelings by acquiring the ideal opposite quality. Today, the unhealthy, clandestine sexual behavior that sometimes surfaces in the lives of lay or clerical "pillars of society" is, more often than not, the result of their psychologically bankrupt religious asceticism. As a philosopher, Whyte understood and could articulate this terrible dilemma. However, at the same time he was unable to offer an effective psychological "process" that could facilitate unitary consciousness. That step had to wait for a more complete understanding of how bodily-felt knowing contributed to human wholeness in the research of Gendlin. Whyte's philosophical contribution, however, was to sow healthy seeds of doubt in the minds of those who could hear what he was saying.

> For all its superb aspiration Christianity has not lessened war, disease, or hatred. It could not, for compassion is dishonest in dissociated man; there is no honesty where unity is lacking . . . Dissociated man has denied his potential unity and lacks the vitality to recover it; he finds balm in the service of others. But the logic of fact is relentless. In rendering his own dissociation tolerable he tends to perpetuate it in others. When self-sacrific-

ing service expresses flight from personal despair it is abortive, for it works to achieve its own doom.[6]

There is impressive evidence to show that our inner conflicts become further actualized and exacerbated when, in order to change, we pursue the ideal opposite of that which we cannot accept within ourselves. The use of such ideals actually thwarts the very transformation they naively are intended to support. Gendlin shows that by penetrating rather than fleeing from feelings of anger, hostility, or other negatively-carried emotions, one eventually can be drawn through to felt meanings that are stuck, allowing them to begin moving forward again. The path to constructive change, therefore, lies through entering into the bodily-felt knowing contained in negative feelings and emotions—feelings which the "ideal" would have us deny, reject, or avoid. "A *good* Christian, parent, priest, etc., would not feel such and such."

The pursuit of ideals puts people who sincerely want to grow in a painful double bind. While being made acutely aware that their attitudes and behavior are in opposition to personal and communal growth, they are at the same time provided with absolutely no way to do anything about the inner blockage which inhibits their movement toward wholeness.

This is the basic weakness of any outside norm such as the pursuit of ideals or obedience to law as a substitute for the "inner dynamic" of grace that heals our brokenness. It is the age-old dilemma of St. Paul:

> I can will what is right, but I cannot do it. For I do not do the good I want, but the evil I do not want is what I do . . . I find it to be a law that when I want to do right, evil lies close at hand . . . Wretched man that I am! Who will deliver me from this body of death? (Rom 7:18-24 RSV)

Law reminds us of our excessively anti-social, egoistic tendencies *but at the same time is incapable of helping us to regenerate our own self-process.* It convicts of sin but in and of itself it is powerless to provide any hope of salvation.

The pursuit of ideals is merely an internalization of this inherent weakness in the law. A dissociated, incongruent person, seeking to grow by pursuing some ideal opposite of whatever negative feeling he or she cannot accept, experiences the same frustrating psychological condition as the apostle Paul.

Most of us have never been instructed that "your sense of what is wrong carries with it, inseparably, a sense of what is right." Even when we are taught this truth of experience, though, most of us still opt to chase the rainbow promise of some alluring ideal. It's so scary to be with your hurt in a gentle, friendly way as we do in Focusing. There is such vulnerability, such loss of control. It's much easier to get involved in the delusion of fixing it yourself.

We do not question the sincerity of so many authors, like the ones referred to in this article who offer exercises and explanations to help people heal their inner pain. But the naivete contained within such exercises and explanations no longer excuses the human suffering and social destructiveness that such practices re-enforce and continue to unleash—albeit in the name of religion. Today, we know better how holiness is gifted in and through the body's process of wholeness. We no longer can risk repeating the mistakes of the past. The stakes now are much too high.

"Process-Skipping"

Focusing helps us to understand the psychological mechanism which locks addictive patterns in place and makes them so resistant to change. We can illustrate the functioning of this mechanism by describing a common experience that provides some sense for what it feels like, on the inside, to live with an addictive way of trying to be present to something.

Have you ever had the maddening experience of pawing through a cluttered kitchen drawer looking for a favorite metal serving spoon mixed in with numerous other utensils, but for the life of you, you just can't see it. Your eye seeks the familiar curved spoon edge but finds nothing, usually because the spoon is partially hidden under other utensils or has gotten jammed on its side so the visual form presented to your eye doesn't match the flat, curved edge you're looking for. Even though physically you may observe it, the spoon doesn't register in awareness as being what you're looking for. *This is because your eye is present primarily to what it expects to see and not to what actually is there.*

Such a common experience can illustrate something of what occurs when addictive patterns become engrained in a person's behavior. Instead of responding with a wholeness of presence to what actually is, the addictive person views life through a complex grid of habit and expectation. Life is reduced to a series of "frozen wholes," as Dr. Gendlin calls them, and the person reacts in terms of these frozen, static structures whether or not they coincide with reality—as, invariably, they do not. Dr. Gendlin says that such a person's experiencing has become *"structure bound."*

We all know about this in one way or another. Each of us has made snap judgments about people because they remind us of someone we don't like, only later to realize that we needed to revise our body-feel for this individual because he or she doesn't fit the pattern we have imposed upon them. A healthy person constantly revises expectations simply by being present to ever-changing reality. People with an addictive pattern locked in place cannot do this. Instead of being in touch with what actually is, their presence is limited by structure-bound patterns that pre-determine what they expect reality to be. Gendlin clearly raises this issue of "presentness" by asking:

> Am I reacting to the present situation? Am I feeling a now, or is the present situation merely an occasion, a cue for a familiar, repetitious, structured pattern of feeling?[7]

Let's illustrate the psychology of addiction by imagining someone who feels excessively guilty about neglecting an aging parent. We are not speaking here of ordinary busy people who fail to make time for their mothers or fathers, but someone who really does do a lot and yet still feels guilty. Rather than getting in touch with unresolved childhood dependancy, for example, or other issues that might underlie the guilt, such a person tries to remove their sense of blame by compulsive attention to his or her parent. Instead of allowing the guilt to dissolve through some process like Focusing on the old sense of not being loved if they don't measure up to what mommy or daddy wanted, for instance, the guilty person tries to assuage the feeling of culpability by directing attention and energy toward taking care of their parent. Every time they feel any twinge of guilt, an automatic, patterned reaction leads them to visit or do something for their parent instead of sitting in a Focusing way with the question: "How does all this guilt and needing to do something for mother or dad feel right now in my body?"

Dr. Gendlin uses the phrase *"process-skipping structure"* to refer to a conditioned reaction which automatically bypasses or obscures the real feelings behind some compulsive, structure-bound pattern and instead substitutes other behavioral responses that seem to relieve the tension, but actually skip by and miss the real source of the problem.

> It seems quite striking and universal that we feel guilt, shame, and badness, instead of feeling that concerning which we feel shame, guilt and badness. It is almost as if these emotions themselves preclude our feeling what it all is to us—not so much because they are so unpleasant, as because they skip the point at which we might complete, symbolize, respond or attend to that which centrally we feel.[8]

The heart of any process-skipping structure is a built-in mechanism which continually diverts attention away from body-feelings that contain the key to changing our compulsive behaviors. The process-skipping structure preserves addiction secure and intact by speeding a person right past the inner turnoff which, if followed, would lead directly toward the resolution of difficult feelings. The excessive guilt over not doing enough for an aging parent is a smokescreen that obscures some deeper experience of, for example, not being loved or somehow never measuring up to our parents' expectations. The underlying story of heartbreak, confusion, loneliness or feelings of inadequacy are, thus, repeatedly drowned in a froth and swirl of guilt that rushes in like the tide to cover all.

One has an illusion of "working with the right thing" when expending energy to care for an aging parent. But the real issue and potential for transformation lie elsewhere. The proof of this is that no matter how devoted a person may be in caring for an aging parent, if the guilt feeling that drives this individual is stuck in an addictive pattern, it will return again and again without ever being satisfied by an episode of "perfect caring." We do not feel our real feelings because part of any addiction is a process-skipping structure that for the most part operates on automatic pilot. Focusing, on the other hand, provides a special key to unlock such structure-bound experience. It brings attention directly to bear upon the body-knowing of loneliness, inadequacy and confusion where there is an immediate potential for process that can effectively dissolve the feeling of guilt.

Although Eugene Gendlin does not directly relate his psychological investigation to addiction, his carefully researched findings about structure-bound experiencing are so applicable that his conclusions provide a striking key to ending the addictive cycle. *The process-skipping structure is what locks addictive patterns in place, making them so resistant to change.* This is fresh evidence and a vital finding that has been missed for quite some time. How this mechanism works and how Focusing brings a person's awareness to the precise point in experiencing where addiction can be dissolved are clear learnings which provide invaluable steps toward recovery. Even more, they highlight crucial ingredients in the development of any "recovery spirituality" for those mired in the trap of religious addictions.

Evaluating "Spiritual" Practices

It is far too easy, today, at retreat and growth centers for many people unknowingly to transfer their addictive behaviors over to so-called "spiritual" practices which are intrinsically incapable of transforming any underlying addictive tendency or pattern. Eventually, restlessness and dissatisfaction will surface all over again, propelling some to seek out alternate practices. Others become "hooked" on a particular approach and cannot cope without it. They keep their troublesome issues and emotions at bay by using the practice over and over again rather than processing their feelings beyond the old stuck places.

A good rule of thumb for evaluating the psychological health of what you practice is simply to stop doing it for awhile and see what happens. Do the old stuck feelings, issues, and memories return to stress you in the same bodily-felt way that they have in the past? Are old patterns and behaviors coming back to haunt you, interfere with work, sleep, relationships, etc.? All this is clear evidence that what you do is a coping, control mechanism—perhaps useful to keep your head above water—but incapable of actually helping you change what is stuck in your body. Are there any clear criteria, then, which we can follow when evaluating the multitude of approaches spawned in response to the rising spiritual hunger of our time? We believe such norms already lie implicit within the Focusing process which offers a carefully nuanced alternative that gets to the heart of what needs to happen for an addictive cycle to be broken. Let's organize our thought around five questions which you can ask yourself about any spiritual or growth practice.

> (1) Does the practice support you in "owning" your feelings, or does it merely make you aware of emotions without helping them to be in process?
>
> (2) Does the practice keep you in touch with your own feelings in a way that allows them to unfold, or does it try to substitute other, more acceptable feelings in place of those that are troublesome?
>
> (3) Is the practice one that actually facilitates change in the feeling of some issue in your body or does it merely provide you with information that affects your ideas and thinking about that issue?
>
> (4) Is the practice one that achieves its effect in you through self-engineering and control or through self-surrender in openness to a process of grace?
>
> (5) When using a practice to grow beyond stuck feelings, is the level of positive change that occurs in the way an issue feels in your body something that endures after the exercise, or must you

keep repeating the practice in order to maintain the level of change that happens?

Question 5 addresses the issue of "coping with" rather than "processing" feelings that continue being carried in the body in a blocked way. Since this needs to be responded to in terms of one's own subjective experience, we will here develop only the first four questions.

1. Does the practice support you in "owning" your feelings or does it merely make you aware of emotions without helping them to be in process?

Owning feelings in your body is different from merely being aware of them. Many spiritual and growth exercises are specifically designed to put you in touch with feelings and this, obviously, is not a bad thing. The problem comes when you are in touch with some strong emotion and then ask the obvious next question: "All right, now what?"

Marriage Encounter

The two of us run into this quandary time and again when speaking with couples who have made a Marriage Encounter weekend. While admitting there were things they learned during the weekend that were helpful and useful, they also candidly share that once their real feelings were out on the table neither knew what to do with them. At that point they became stuck and could go no further. The Marriage Encounter Movement recognizes an obvious importance in honestly sharing feelings. What it lacks, though, is some practical process that helps couples be with their feelings in a way that allows them to unfold and change into something better. The question is, how do you get in touch with powerful feelings, particularly those that are negative, without becoming stuck and merely wallowing or going about in an endless circle with them? Marriage Encounter talks about feelings but has no body-process of actually owning difficult emotions so they can change.

This is where Focusing offers a practical alternative as well as a far more sophisticated explanation that can help you better understand *the actual process of change.* Focusing teaches you to "own" your feelings by differentiating between emotion and a "felt sense" which is the way in which your body carries felt meaning. A felt sense is your *embodied* way of knowing some person, situation, thing or event. It's not a mental experience but a *physical* one. The felt sense includes but is always more than any single emotion. If, for example, you and a close friend have an argument, your predominant emotion concerning this friend may be anger.

But your felt sense of that person is far more complex—including all your body sense for the good times as well as more recent difficult days. It is the broader felt sense and not merely the emotion which needs to be "owned," listened to and allowed to tell you what it knows. Yet, the felt sense never exists in total isolation from the emotion.

This is where Gendlin made a very significant finding. He learned how an "emotion" relates to a "felt sense" and how the process of Focusing helps us avoid being overcome by and wallowing in our feelings. The following illustration describes the difference between felt sense, or felt meaning, and an emotion.

> . . . the preoccupation with . . . emotions is not to be confused with the felt meaning which, though connected to these emotions, needs the focusing.
>
> One client describes it in terms of a hurricane: "If you only go so far into something, it's like going into a hurricane and getting terribly blown around. You have to go into it and then keep going further and further in till you get to the eye of the hurricane. There it's quiet and you can see where you are." *This beautifully expresses the fact that the direction of focusing is definitely into the emotions, not away from them, yet also that focusing involves something qualitatively very different than merely "being blown around" by the emotions.* (emphasis ours)[9]

Owning your feelings is the same as being congruent with them. That means being able consciously to feel your feelings physiologically and to allow them to symbolize themselves accurately. The clarifications which Gendlin introduces through Focusing are the precise way you move beyond merely being blown around by your emotion.

> . . . to turn away from the emotion is to turn away also from the direction in which one "finds oneself." Thus, one must "move into" and "through," or "on by," these emotional tones to the . . . felt meaning of it all. (emphasis ours)[10]

The felt sense is reached through the emotion, never when bypassing it. Congruence, or "owning," is the disciplined process of entering into and moving through an emotion to the bodily-felt sense which lies beyond. So often in Marriage Encounter, spiritual guidance or support groups one finds exercises that put people in touch with feelings and encourage them to share or talk about those feelings. But if the exercise does not help them to "own" such feelings, then it has only taken a first step which is never adequate in itself. Often, just being in touch with feelings creates a potentially dangerous situation where relationships can be damaged rather than healed and individuals become discouraged about contacting feelings that remain so painful when no resolution or change occurs.

Focusing teaches *the process* of "moving into and through" the emotions. This is an important learning about how feelings change.

2. Does the practice keep you in touch with your own feelings in a way that allows them to unfold, or does it seek to substitute other more acceptable feelings in place of those that are troublesome?

The common approach followed by most people in their quest for change is to embody some ideal that is the opposite of what they find unacceptable in themselves. There are, however, variations on this theme that also need critically to be evaluated. Sometimes, without even noticing it, subtle elements of this approach can work their way into exercises that otherwise might be quite useful.

Centering Prayer

For example, Centering Prayer as developed by Father Basil Pennington offers a simple way to grow quiet inside and seek the presence of God within the core of one's being. This popular approach draws upon a little book called *The Cloud of Unknowing*, written by a nameless English Catholic writer of the fourteenth century. The prayer incorporates elements quite similar to those of the Jesus Prayer. After a period of preparatory quieting and meditation, it includes the repetitive use of a simple word like "God" or "Love" which is recited over and over again as a means of simplifying one's attention and resting in the Presence of God within one's heart or center.

There are three basic "rules" associated with this prayer technique which Fr. Pennington summarizes in his book, all the while carefully emphasizing that no approach to contemplative prayer can ever adequately be expressed through a set of rules. Nonetheless, the rules do help highlight a very essential difference between Centering Prayer and Focusing. The third rule gives directions that are potentially process-skipping.

> Rule One: At the beginning of the prayer we take a minute or two to quiet down and then move in faith to God dwelling in our depths; and at the end of the prayer we take several minutes to come out, mentally praying the 'Our Father.'

> Rule Two: After resting for a bit in the center in faithful love, we take up a single, simple word that expresses this response and begin to let it repeat itself within.
>
> Rule Three: Whenever in the course of the prayer we become aware of anything else, we simply gently return to the prayer word.[11]

It is the Third Rule which calls for our attention. This is the one that deals with distractions. Centering prayer, according to Fr. Pennington, is intended to move one below thoughts and images into one's center. But daily cares and worries often pull us back from such a depth of communion. The Third Rule is intended to remedy this.

> In this prayer we go below the thoughts and images offered by the mind and imagination. But at times they will grab at our attention and try to draw it away from the restful Presence. This is because these thoughts or images refer to something that has a hold on us, something we fear, or desire, or are in some other way intensely involved with. When we become aware of these thoughts, if we continue to dwell on them, we leave our prayer and become involved again in the tensions. But if, at the moment of awareness, we simply, gently return to our prayer word (thus implicitly renewing our act of presence in faith-full love), the thought or image with its attendant tension will be released and flow out of our lives. And we will come into a greater freedom and peace that will remain after our prayer is over.[12]

Centering Prayer recognizes the potential hazard in emotion, the distracting power that is there. Its solution, though, is not to go deeper into and through the tension feeling of the distraction itself in the search for communion with God. Rather, the "prayer word" is introduced as a way of bringing the one in prayer back to his or her center.

Focusing, by contrast, brings us to a congruent centering which can be experienced only as one surrenders to being drawn into and through some troublesome tension or emotion to the felt meaning beyond—all of which is gift, a grace, an act of faith. Most "distractions" tell us something very important about priorities and what currently needs to be "owned," "listened to" and not run away from right now. Whatever comes in a bodily-felt way to "distract" us from prayer is more than likely a uniquely personal doorway into the Mystery of God precisely because it is a special doorway into ourselves. *Pulling away from the realism of this embodied experience by returning to some word that brings calm, peace, quiet and love is the real distraction!*

Focusing helps us realize that the very experience we consider distracting, fear most in ourselves, or view as a block to serenity, inner quiet, and even God is actually our most precious doorway into the peace and presence of God. It is a point of entry given when we risk "owning" the truth of ourselves as one more step into wholeness.

Sometimes, people tell us that Centering Prayer taught them to grow quiet inside and that this made it easier to learn Focusing. Our reason for discussing this type of prayer is not to question its benefits, but to alert those using it to the potential problem of inserting a process-skipping structure into one's prayer. This precision must be emphasized because, over the centuries, in far too many instances Christian devotional practice has fueled the "dissociative" tendency with tragic consequences, as L. L. Whyte has clearly pointed out. We have reached a point in history where each of us can begin taking responsibility for reversing this destructive pattern. Focusing invites us into a very real "Cloud of Unknowing," the felt-sense with all its mystery, wonder, terror and awesome potential to lead us home to our true selves in God.

3. Is the practice one that actually facilitates change in the feeling of some issue in your body or does it merely provide you with information that affects your ideas and thinking about that issue?

Sufi Enneagram

A further illustration may help us appreciate how Focusing provides clear guidelines when we take a critical look at spiritual practices. The Sufi Enneagram is described as representing a "journey into self." It is proposed as a way of discovering one's own personality type among the nine which comprise this particular system. Teachers of this approach claim that there is a compulsion or basic driving force associated with each of the types. The compulsion is seen as a defensive strategy developed by the person in order to find a secure and meaningful existence. The negative side effect of such compulsion, however, is that it induces a kind of paralysis and hinders the discovery of one's true self. Personal growth in the Enneagram system involves "acting against the compulsion." This requires personal effort.

> It is an *agere contra*, an 'acting against.' One moves contrary to the inner inclination of the compulsion. The Enneagram provides a clear "map" of the direction for each personality type.[13]

Perhaps this is an accurate analysis, but an important question needs to be asked as one examines this "clear map" and the direction it indicates:

How? How does one move toward the ideal opposite of a compulsive personality characteristic? Unless the system in question can provide a practical answer to such a simple question, then, ultimately, of what benefit is it? Gendlin pinpoints the missing link in this kind of personality theory when he notes that there is:

> . . . a trouble with most concepts about personality change and psychotherapy as well as with most concepts of ideals, moral values, and life wisdom. The concepts tell us a little something of how it seems when one has arrived at the (goal), *but they tell nothing of the process of getting there.* [emphasis ours] Such concepts make all sorts of mischief because we tend to try to fit them without allowing ourselves the very different process of getting there.[14]

The illusion behind much of this futile activity is that if we can better *understand* and analyze our situation or predicament somehow it will help us to change.

Personality disorders may be assessed from as many different vantage points as there are typologists to make such assessments. But in the last analysis, if the system can only tell us where to go without at the same time providing concrete tools for "the very different process of getting there," then of what real benefit is all the effort expended to learn the system? This question needs to be asked over and over again. Why should anyone invest valuable time and energy in a spiritual or growth program that fails to deliver the goods? Theoretical analysis is fine. Information can be valuable. The benefits of people coming together for a weekend workshop are often quite productive. There is an obvious benefit in learning something about how people are different. We think, act and respond in diverse ways and it is useful to recognize and respect this. *But none of this informational analysis actually helps us to change! At best, it merely alerts us to the fact that maybe we need to change.*

Focusing is very specific and concrete in its response to the question "How?" If there is an important or troublesome issue, invariably it is felt in the body. One takes time to sit in a caring, gentle way with the body-feel of that issue, both surface emotion as well as the more complex felt meaning that surrounds and supports it. In time, the felt meaning will symbolize itself, moving forward in a shift that can be sensed throughout the entire organism. One does not direct effort and attention toward some ideal opposite of the bodily-felt issue as a way of balancing it out, gaining control over, or changing it. Neither does one seek distraction as a means of escape. Criteria like these need careful considering, especially by retreat house directors and spiritual guides.

Another informational trip we often lay on ourselves is what Gendlin describes as a *"circumstantial orbit."* Just as we can get lost in feelings so, too, we easily become mired in an endless inner recitation of all the circumstances surrounding some difficult experience. We go into great detail about what we should have done or said, replaying conversations over and over again. It's fascinating to note how people re-live their conversations. "He said . . ., and then she said . . . and I said . . ." Such re-spinning of old tapes totally misses the underlying felt meanings that need to be sat with in a Focusing way. Instead of directing attention toward some concrete body-felt knowing that surrounds a particular issue, the process-skipping dead-end of reciting endless circumstances pulls awareness away from our bodies and rivets attention on an effort to rewrite history.

Those involved in "support groups" need to be alert for the pitfalls associated with this kind of useless chatter. People get worked up recalling details surrounding their painful episodes without at the same time making any significant progress toward resolving their feelings about an issue. Unless the recalling of some circumstance puts a person in touch with here and now felt-meaning that can then be focused on, a great deal of energy is expended without ever getting anywhere.

Another dead-ended approach to change is what Gendlin refers to as the *"explanatory orbit."* This is a further variation on the theme of substituting information for actual Focusing and occurs when we try to figure out why we are the way we are as a way to change.

> Whether the explanatory concepts are simple and foolish or sophisticated and quite correct, they are useless unless one employs them as pointers to momentarily name and hold onto a directly felt meaning. Without that, one cogitates in a vacuum and gets 'no further.' The explanatory 'runaround' races the mental engine, disengaged from the wheels. It makes one tired and confused, and it is quite different from focusing on the felt meaning. Even one small step of the focusing process can change the inner scene so that one's whole set of explanatory concepts suddenly becomes irrelevant. In comparison with the felt meaning, explanatory concepts are so gross, so general, so empty, that even when they are accurate they are helpless abstractions.[15]

Two helpful criteria stand out in this statement of Gendlin's. He clearly differentiates explanatory concepts from "the process of getting there." This is important data when learning systems of personality theory as, for example, Jung's description of the Archetypes. Such theoretical information is never the same as an actual experience of "individuation." *It can never be emphasized enough that knowing information is not the process of human wholeness.*

Gendlin also adds a helpful insight about how explanations can be at the service of inner process. This happens not because of their abstract intellectual content (the information they impart), but insofar as the explanation helps an individual directly refer in a Focusing way to some aspect of his or her current felt experiencing that needs to be symbolized and move forward.

4. Is the practice one that achieves its effect in you through self-engineering and control, or through self-surrender and openness to a process of grace?

Self-engineering occurs whenever we talk at ourselves, trying to fix or rearrange our feelings without ever becoming congruent with them. Efforts like this usually include a great deal of willpower and decision-making with little or no processing of what is going on inside ourselves. Such out-of-touchness has become so much part of our culture and romantic folk lore that we scarcely recognize when it is being slipped in to influence us and, more significantly, our children. Just read the words of this popular song from *The Sound of Music.*

> When the dog bites, when the bee stings,
> When I'm feeling sad,
> I simply remember my favorite things
> and then I don't feel so bad.[16]

The lyrics, of course, are charming. The melody memorable in its lighthearted whimsy. But the mental health message is definitely off base. Remembering one's favorite things as a way of alleviating stress is just one more tired form of self-engineering. There is some merit in positive thinking. But in and of itself *it does not process negative feelings.* People easily become addicted to positive thinking as a substitute for processing the difficult feelings they carry. Occasionally, we attend lectures or listen to tapes in which the speaker spells out some theoretical position, often in a clear and excellent fashion. Then follows "an exercise" intended to lead the audience through some sort of experiential "process." The clash, on occasion, between brilliant analysis and the inappropriateness of a chosen exercise with which to illustrate and embody this information can be striking.

Developing Personal Boundaries

Therapist John Bradshaw, for example, has excellent things to say about the need for boundaries and the role of shame in dysfunctional families. His information is clear and provocative. The examples and his own personal experience are right on target. One set of tapes on "Developing Personal Boundaries" includes perceptive comments on religious addictions. Bradshaw notes that this is the most prevalent problem he deals with in therapy. Clients, in his words, "avoid their reality by being addicted to religion." Interestingly, he notes that one of the commonalities within incest-abusing families is strict religious adherence and upbringing. He has found that the amount of shame and guilt built up within such addictive environments is enormous.

On occasion during his lectures, Bradshaw will lead his audience through various exercises as a way of helping them develop better personal boundaries or deal with guilt and shame over past experiences. Based on our research and experience, certain of his exercises, unfortunately, do not support the processing of negative feelings even though they may somewhat modify behavior. The bottom line, however, is that such activity does not facilitate a development of congruence which is the solid base upon which lasting change can be built. For example, during one lecture on "Developing Personal Boundaries," Bradshaw included an exercise borrowed from Jack Schwarz as a way of helping a person develop an inner boundary which no outsider could violate. After a series of progressive relaxation exercises, Bradshaw led his audience into some inward imagining in which they pictured themselves walking down a long corridor and into a brightly lit room. Participants in his workshop were encouraged to "paint" this room in their favorite colors and fill it with the special furniture they liked the best. This was a room where no one else could go, an inner sanctuary to which they could retire whenever they wanted. Special emphasis was placed on filling the room with favorite sounds and special odors that meant something to the one involved in the exercise. Every effort was made to include all the senses.

Bradshaw then told his audience that this was a secure place where they could go and be with their higher power. He suggested that they invite their higher power into the room and feel themselves surrounded with light. Every part of their person was so surrounded, like an armor or shield. He then had his participants leave their special rooms in their imagination and go outside this secure space, but with the light of the higher power still surrounding them. Once outside the room, Bradshaw had them touch their thumb and forefinger when they could feel themselves surrounded by the power. He then suggested that: "Every time you touch your thumb and finger you can feel this boundary. It's like being warm and snug under the covers of your bed." Afterwards, he led them out of the exercise with an encouragement to practice feeling this secure boundary and sense of their higher power whenever they touched their thumb and finger. The idea being that every time they brought these two fingers together in a stressful situation where their boundaries were under attack, they would physically bring back the memory and sense of this inner secure wall of protection. The exercise was presented and intended as a way to integrate some of the more theoretical information covered in the lectures.

But is this really a "process" in the sense of a practice that helps move congruence forward or is it merely an imaginative exercise with little or no transforming connection to the issue of personal boundaries and shame?

What we observe here is a clear exercise in self-engineering which, in the name of wholeness, deliberately erects a process-skipping structure as the basis for transforming an inadequate sense of self. Fear, shame, feelings of being violated—whatever is there—is never allowed to tell its story and be heard. As soon as negative emotions are felt, the one meditating deliberately pushes a process-skipping button to create an 'inner room of light and feeling of security.' Even though this is a deliberately manipulated effect, the outcome is the same as when such a structure automatically goes into effect—like guilt over neglecting an aging parent that pulls us away from some feeling of inadequacy or not measuring up. It's the "My Favorite Things" honey-coating repeated over and over again.

When saying this we in no way fault Bradshaw for failing to deal with important issues. Indeed, as mentioned earlier, some of his perceptive insights and personal experience are so useful for helping others to understand shame, guilt and the need for personal boundaries, that we believe it is vital for his message to be heard. We only want to show that Focusing helps us develop more accurate criteria for assessing exercises intended to deal with shame, guilt or any other negative feeling. *The direction toward wholeness and self-process is always into and through the negative emotion that most people spend their lives running away from.*

Moreover, there is a deeper issue here—a spiritual one. All this self-engineering never teaches a process of surrender, a letting go of manipulation and disposing of ourselves for grace—even when this is done with the kindest of intent and most tranquil of means. Control is control, whether done gently with soft whispering or through ruthless determination. Carl Rogers once said that the only real security for a growing person is the stability of process. Boundaries are developed not by creating snug little nests of warm security but through discovering a sense of moving forward in your life.

Self-engineering deadens our sensitivity to grace. It is a beguiling prospect—to gain power over your adversary—yet the gospel message opens a radically different approach to human transformation. "But I say to you: Love your enemies and pray for those who persecute you." (Mt.5:44 RSV) In Focusing we learn how to love that part of ourselves we have made into the enemy. An important aspect of Eugene Gendlin's contribution is to help us appreciate the psychology of how grace operates within the human organism.

"Owning" the felt sense by moving into and on through emotions

One difficulty we encountered early in our teaching of Focusing was the problem people had when moving into emotions and felt meanings that were scary for them. Those in the habit of avoiding painful feelings found it extremely difficult to be in and move through feelings from which they invariably sought escape. Gendlin tried to soften the trauma by teaching a technique called "distancing." How far away from the bad feeling did one need to remain in order to risk feeling it?

Gendlin systematically tried to help a person stay in touch with the painful feeling but at a sufficiently removed distance so they could bear being with it. He even suggested imaginative exercises such as putting the bad feeling in a bag and placing it on the other side of the room. This was helpful on some occasions, but didn't seem to go far enough in our view. Often, for example, we found that people would become very involved in the exercise of "packaging" their difficult feeling. So caught up did they become, in fact, that we frequently found them using the exercise as one more way of distracting themselves from Focusing.

What eventually worked for us was teaching people to have a *"caring-feeling-presence"* toward the feelings they wanted to push away. This became an important contribution in our workshops and eventually a key ingredient in teaching people how to "own" their feelings. We soon realized, however, that "caring-feeling-presence" could not simply be willed into existence. It was not an attitude of the mind but, rather, a visceral way of being with an issue that physically felt quite different from the usual approach people had of pushing hurt feelings away. Each individual, we found, had to discover his or her unique manner of "being friendly" with whatever they usually held at arm's length.

Imagery can help this process as, for example, by holding one's pain like one might hold a hurting child. It is important, physiologically, to feel some kind of caring connection with what previously has been pushed away. Sometimes, just using a word like "caring," "gentle," "open" can tone the quality of presence. Even performing a physical act like placing your hand in a caring way on the location in your body where you feel pain most acutely (whether physical or psychological) can be helpful. Occasionally, just the attitude of being with a hurting place as "teacher" rather than "enemy" is sufficient.

Moving into and through feelings toward the deeper felt meaning of it all is an important part of "owning" and of "congruence" as we have described them. "Caring-feeling-presence" is our way of supporting this movement in a person. We find that it has less chance of distracting an individual from deeper feelings that need to be sat with in a Focusing way. This open, caring bodily-felt presence to inner feelings and meanings is a crucial ingredient in breaking the cycle of addiction.

In summary, then, it is important to realize how every addiction includes its own self-locking mechanism which makes it almost impervious to change. There is an in-built smoke-screen deluding an addictive person into imagining that he or she is coming to grips with negative behavior and compulsions, when in actual fact they are being led further astray. Anne Wilson Schaef perceptively describes this confusing situation.

> An addiction keeps us unaware of what is going on inside us. We do not have to deal with our anger, pain, depression, confusion, or even our joy and love because we do not feel them, or we feel them only vaguely. We stop relying on our knowledge and our sense and start relying on our confused perceptions to tell us what we know and sense. In time, this lack of internal awareness deadens our internal processes, which in turn allows us to remain addicted . . . An addiction dulls and distorts our sensory input. We do not receive information clearly; we do not process it accurately; and we do not feed it back or respond to it with precision. Since we are not in touch with ourselves, we present a distorted self to the world—in terms of Alcoholics Anonymous (AA) we "con" people—and eventually lose the ability to become intimate with others, even those we are closest to and love the most.[17]

Unfortunately, a good deal of "conning" is built right into the very approaches we use to grow and change. Self-engineering, the naive confusing of imaginative meditation exercises with self-process, or the deliberate avoidance of entering into difficult emotions in order to move through them to felt meaning that lies beyond—all these are ways in which "conning" gets built into our sincerest desire to change. An important part of becoming better informed about addiction is learning more about self-process and how to sniff out conning that is already built into the "spiritual growth" exercise itself.

Endnotes

1. Eugene T. Gendlin, *Focusing*. New York, Everest House, 1978, p. 75.

2. *Loc. Cit.*

3. Eddie Ensley, *Prayer that Heals our Emotions*. Columbus, Contemplative Books, 1986, p. 74-75.

4. Lancelot Law Whyte, *The Next Development in Man*. New York, New American Library (Mentor Edition), 1948. p. 254.

5. *Ibid.*, p.203.

6. *Ibid.*, p.204.

7. Eugene T. Gendlin, "A Theory of Personality Change," in Philip Worchel and Don Byrne, Eds., *Personality Change*. New York, John Wiley & Sons, 1964, p. 127.

8. *Ibid.*, p.123.

9. Eugene T. Gendlin, *Op.Cit.*, p. 124.

10. *Loc.Cit.*

11. M. Basil Pennington, O.C.S.O., *Daily We Touch Him—Practical Religious Experiences*. New York, Doubleday & Company, Inc. (Image Book Edition), 1979. pp. 58, 66, 68.

12. *Ibid.*, pp. 68, 69.

13. Maria Beesing, O.P., Robert J. Nogosek, C.S.C., Patrick H. O'Leary, S.J., *The Enneagram: A Journey of Self-Discovery*. New Jersey, Dimension Books, Inc., 1984, p. 157.

14. Eugene T. Gendlin, "A Theory of Personality Change," in Philip Worchel and Don Byrne, Eds., *Personality Change*. New York, John Wiley & Sons, 1964, p. 134.

15. *Ibid.*, p.125.

16. "My Favorite Things" from *The Sound of Music*, words by Oscar Hammerstein II, music by Richard Rodgers.

17. Anne Wilson Schaef, "We're a Nation of Addicts," in *New Age Journal*, March/April 1987, p. 43.

Notes

Notes

About the Authors

Fathers Edwin M. McMahon, Ph.D. and ***Peter A. Campbell, Ph.D.*** have found that the experience of grace in the body can heal addictive behaviors that destory community. Their workshops and writings show that systems of dominance and codependence can be transformed by the body-experience of grace. They have conducted psychological research for 34 years in order to understand how religious practices contribute to health or pathology. Focusing, which they teach, offers a healthy, simple, practical process for being in touch with body-knowing. It is easily taught to children and quickly becomes a powerful, nurturing support for the development of human wholeness and healthy relationships.

Drs. Campbell and McMahon are co-directors of the Institute for Bio-Spiritual Research, authors, workshop and retreat leaders who conduct programs in Bio-Spirituality through Focusing. Their books include *Becoming a Person in the Whole Christ, The In-Between: Evolution in Christian Faith, Please Touch*, and *Bio-Spirituality: Focusing as a Way to Grow.* Other materials include a series of booklets (as well as audiotapes and videotapes) now published by Sheed & Ward.

Please note:

The authors, the Institute for Bio-Spiritual Research, and the publishers, do not teach Focusing or promote Focusing Companions either as a substitute for professional psychotherapeutic or psychiatric care for those who need it, or as a substitute for training and licensing in the above health fields.

Complete List of Focusing Resources

1. What Is Focusing?
2. What Is "Spiritual" About Focusing
3. The Focusing Steps
4. Questions Often Asked About Focusing and Spirituality
5. The Inward Connection
6. Teaching Children to Focus
7. Focusing and Prayer
8. Childhood Wonder
9. Searching for God With Our Fingertips
10. The Grace of Forgiving Yourself Through Focusing
11. Addictive Religion
12. Focusing and Self-Renewal
13. A Woman's Prayer
14. "Process Skipping:" Mechanisms That Lock In Addictive Patterns
15. A Bio-Spiritual Approach to Sexuality
16. Journeying Together in Spirit
17. How Adults Can Listen to Children in a Focusing Way
18. Focusing: Doorway to the Body-Life of Spirit
19. Focusing Companions: New Model for Relationships

Video Resources

1. Focusing and Bio-Spirituality
2. Because It Works
3. Focusing Companions (Part 1)
4. Focusing Companions (Part 2)
5. Focusing Companions (Part 3): New Model for Community

Video Sets

(A) Spirituality and Focusing
(B) Focusing Companions
(C) Complete Introductory Set